I0471237

Copyright 2013 Elliot Publishing LLC

Preface

Men--this book contains everything the government doesn't want you to know. The government wants you to think the Child Support System has spiritual meaning, is fair and reasonable, and, above all, has moral purpose. However, the truth about this system is a far cry from what you are led to believe, and it is vital to your financial survival that you full grasp the true nature of the System.

For those in the know, the system can be used for their personal advantage. If you are willing to join them, this book will guide you. *The Child Support Trap* offers you a twelve-step process to understanding how to beat the system, or at least gain   a degree of control of your life before the System destroys you or lands you in jail.

Most importantly, this book is written for all men embroiled in Child Support System, as well as all men who need to protect themselves from the System. This book is not for scholars, but for everyone regardless of their profession or education. Just follow the process and at the end, you have a chance to achieve financial survival for the benefit of yourself and your children survive. This book offers no guarantees, only direction.

Best of Luck,

Alan W. Cohen, J.D.
August 8, 2012

I. TWELVE STEPS TO SURVIVING THE CHILD SUPPORT SYSTEM

War is not only about winning and losing, it is about survival. In order to survive, you must know the rules of the playing field. No playing field is more filled with proverbial land mines than the Child Support System. The system is filled with false promises and shocking surprises. The twelve-step process is your guide to understanding the false promises and learning how to avoid those land mines. At the end, we will review the answers to the ten keys to survival. Thus, before proceeding with the twelve steps to understanding how to avoid the Child Support Trap, take a few minutes to ask yourself these questions:.

1. How can I plan out a successful strategy?
2. What background information do I need to obtain to build a successful strategy?
3. What is the outcome that I want, and what is the outcome that will help me survive?
4. How can get my mind right to follow a successful strategy?
5. What information about the other parties do I need to build a survival strategy?
6. What resources should I use to build and carry out a successful plan?
7. What information do I need to make a deal with the other parties that would be in my best interest?
8. How will my financial status, and the financial status of the other party, affect my strategy?

9. What formula should I use to formulate my strategy?

10. Once I have formulated a survival strategy, how do I carry it out?

STEP ONE:
Acceptance

"When it comes to the law, nothing is understood."

Dragline, in "Cool Hand Luke"

Men. Empty your minds of what you think you know about the child support system and accept you know nothing. Forget everything you've heard on the street, from your friends and neighbors, from your coworkers, other professionals and even your religious leaders. In order to grasp the complexity of the system, you must be a blank slate.

History shows what is right and wrong changes from generation to generation. There's a great deal of smoke and mirrors. If you believe doing what you consider to be right will bring you salvation, then this book is no help to you. You will do what you want regardless of what I say. If you are following your core beliefs, or that of your religion, and believe God will protect you in the end, remember that God helps those who help themselves.

So clear your mind and read on and learn what the government has not been willing to tell you.

STEP TWO:
Understanding How the System Works

"For every complex problem, there is an answer that is clear, simple and wrong."

H.L. Mencken

The stated goal of the child support system is to establish paternity and to collect support for the "best interest of the child," but this is simple justification. The truth set out in many court cases is to protect the government's bank accounts. Every time the government doles out funds, it seeks someone to reimburse those funds. The problem of course is that more than 99 percent of the cost of the system is not reimbursable under the law. Yet, the system continues to find more and more ways to grab power and violate personal rights.

The system works like this: The federal government pays out welfare to states. In exchange for these funds, the states have to agree to pass certain laws the federal government dictates to obtain reimbursement, or to prevent payment of welfare to its citizens. Under this agreement, since 1997, each state was required to change its law to make it easier to establish paternity of children born out of wedlock. The idea was to allow the mother and alleged father to sign a document at the hospital of birth that would forever bind fathers (absent a high level of proof in a court case) to their admission of paternity.

Under this agreement, with federal funding, each state has two levels of adjudication, the administrative level and the judicial level. The federal government prefers the administrative level because it is allegedly the fastest and most efficient. The state administrative level is usually called Child Support Enforcement. Each parent, regardless of whether anyone is receiving public assistance, has the right to ask the administrative office to assist in the collection of child support. The minute this occurs, the Child Support System is engaged.

An administrative agency has the authority to establish a child support order only if there is no prior court order for support, and:

- The parents are married and separated; or
- The parents have signed the birth affidavit acknowledging paternity; or
- The parents have had DNA testing establishing that the father

is more than 98 percent likely to be the natural father.

An administrative agency does not have the authority to award custody, but it has the authority to find that a child is residing mostly with one parent or the other.

For almost forty years, the primary tool of the child support system has run through the local prosecuting attorney's office. The federal government provides funding to the states to create and support a separate staff to establish paternity/support orders in civil court and to enforce all child support orders in both civil and criminal courts. At first, enforcement was primarily through civil contempt, but federal pressure twenty years ago added the threat of felony charges against non-payers. The prosecutor's office has odd powers and limitations. This office can only:

- Accept cases received as referrals from administrative child support agencies (even those from other states).

- Prosecute criminal non-support cases received from the local administrative agency.
- Represent the state agency in establishing paternity/support orders (and not the person seeking support).

Once the prosecutor's office has the case in hand, it has an incredible amount of discretion to settle or dispose of the case. In this the office can:

- Settle any child support establishment case on its own terms without consulting the parent receiving support.
- Decide whether to file any court action it chooses to enforce, and decide how to adjudicate it (dismissing, settling, or taking the matter to trial).

How the System Has Changed

The Child Support System is fifty years old as of 2012, but persists as if it were still 1962.

Before the 1960s, each state made up its own rules about what we call family law. We had fifty states (as of 1959) and fifty different rules. The fact is the federal government wanted no part in family law. In fact, the federal courts had a long history of refusing to hear family law cases. So each state's high court determined its own law.

In 1962, for many, the biggest legal problem was children born outside of marriage. Many states adopted the law that had been in place since colonial days-- if a woman had a baby and wasn't married, well shame on her. The baby was her problem, and her responsibility. Her chastity was hers to protect. If the natural father wished to acknowledge the child as his, that was fine, but the law could not force him. The purpose of this law was to preserve the sanctity of marriage. Even if the mother was married to someone who was not the natural father of her child, the child was strongly presumed to be her husband's. And, of course, no real man would admit if his wife's infant child were not his own. Again, the purpose was to preserve the institution of marriage.

In England, the birthplace of colonial law, the law of paternity was whether they had the right to inherit the family title and fortune. From Colonial times through 1962, states embraced the right to inheritance and labeled all those children born out of wedlock as "bastards," or children who were not entitled to their father's inheritance. Before sometime in post-World War II America, children were created, not as dependents, but as laborers. The question, especially when it came to sons, was whether the right to inherit. The duty of the father to support his children, while always present, was secondary.

Unintended Consequences

In 1962, the John F. Kennedy administration devised what was thought to be a brilliant solution. Welfare cost was killing the budget, as more and more potential taxpayers were on the public dole. During this time, 23.7 percent of all spending went to welfare programs while 28.3 percent of the working population did not pay taxes. After all, this was the land of opportunity. Jobs were there for the industrious. Only the lazy, the drunk, or the useless did not support their families. So, the Kennedy administration changed the rules. Women could only receive public assistance if the man did not live in the home.

In 1962, it was *Leave it to Beaver* world. The husband typically went to work, and the wife stayed home and played the role of the dutiful wife and mother. The time of working together as a family unit was all but gone, except for family farms or family businesses. So, the roles were well defined. Husbands earned the money. Wives raised the children. This idea was so engrained with the states, that state courts adopted the "Tender Years Presumption," —finding that any child seven or younger should reside with his or her mother even if their father was the better parent.

This new policy of giving money only to women without men residing in the house had many unintended consequences, one being a virtual explosion in the cost of the welfare system in the mid-1960s. As explained in the next step, the government has been trying to fix the mistake ever since, including the creation of the child support system.

STEP THREE:
Acceptance of Immorality

The Child Support System is a bureaucracy with no conscience, compassion, understanding or humanity. The System is about money, and justification of the use of Federal power.

The Child Support System is a rare combination of a process that is stuck in the past while being tangled up in modern technology and surveillance.

Although the thoughtful intention in 1962 was for the system to save money, the result was, in fact, the very opposite. In 1964, Professor Daniel Patrick Moynihan, later a senator from New York, performed a study to discover why. His findings illuminated that attempting to seek reimbursement was a fruitless waste of money because poor children usually meant poor fathers, and a vast majority could not afford to support their children. Moynihan's report found the change in policy in fact caused irreversible harm to the poor families it was supposed to help. Therefore, Moynihan recommended a reversal of the 1962 decision to limit AFDC to single-parent families.

In politics, unlike the field of science, if politicians don't get the answer you are looking for in a commissioned study, they ignore the findings and commission another study. For the next twelve years, study after study confirmed Moynihan's original findings. Finally, the government made the decision to do the one thing it could do—cease funding for the studies.

Before making the decision to decommission the studies, the government continued on its original course seeking reimbursement of benefits. Government continued on this course even though the percentage it received was less than one percent of the cash benefit. In fact, during this same period, the Johnson administration was greatly expanding the possible benefits. Rather than just cash, the government was now offering Medicaid, food stamps, and housing, with other benefit programs to come-- all in the name of fighting poverty. According to the Moynihan study, the opposite was true and the policy only served to increase the number of single-parent, and thus poorer, households; however, politics is about justification, not truth, and is certainly not about morality.

As is often the case in politics, they needed a fall guy, someone with no political power, to blame and justify its costs. They found their fall guy and gave him an appropriate name-- the Deadbeat Dad.

The Perfect Storm

In 1962, the percentage of children born to unmarried women was less than five percent, closer to three percent. Today, the percentage is almost 50 percent. Some blame the relaxing divorce laws. Some blame the free love era of the 60s and 70s. Others blame the "me" generation of the 70s.

But, while there is no smoking gun, the truth can be found in a brief of a 1968 Supreme Court case, *Levy v. Louisiana*. At issue was whether children born out of wedlock were entitled to Equal Protection, in that case, the right to inherit or collect death benefits, as were children born during a lawful marriage. As discussed earlier, the Supreme Court had, until the 1960s, stayed out of family law. States, many argued, had the right to make this call.

But for our purposes, the question of the day is why the virtual explosion of children born to unwed mothers? The answer, according to the Attorney General for Louisiana, falls squarely with the federal government and its inane policy change in 1962. He argued that after the policy change, the percentage of out-of-wedlock children had increased to more than five percent because the Welfare System had directly increased the percentage of single-parent households. He argued that, if the Supreme Court granted equal rights to these children, it would lead to the death of marriage in the United States. The legendary Nostradamus couldn't have seen the future any clearer.

Today, we not only have a crisis in the institution of marriage, but parenthood is now defined as whether the sperm hit the egg, at least as the Child Support System defines it, and sometimes not even then. Sometimes the System defines a parent as one who (foolishly or mistakenly) signed the birth "affidavit" at the hospital, or one who was "legally served with process" but did not respond in a timely manner. In the end, in the eyes of the System, parenthood, at least fatherhood, is the determination that someone is financially responsible. Nothing else matters, and if you are one who the system has wrongly declared financially responsible-- get yourself a good lawyer.

In 1962, 23 percent of Americans were receiving public assistance. In 2010, that number was 45 percent. In 1962, public assistance was 28.3 percent of the federal budget. In 2010, 70.5 percent of the federal budget went to public assistance.

So, how can the federal government justify the child support system? Simple, it continues to blame the Deadbeat Dads.

STEP FOUR:
Find Your
Moral Compass

Morality is what society thinks is right, and what society thinks is right, or wrong, is an ever-moving needle on a compass. In the Judeo-Christian world, the Muslim world, or any other world that believes in an afterlife, morality is how God will judge you after you are dead. Look at the issues of abortion, gay marriage, plural marriage, sex outside of marriage, divorce, even contraception. In the past fifty years, the needle has moved so many times on the compass, it is difficult to point to true north. Some believe abortion is murder--period. Others believe homosexuality is a sin. Others find a moral middle ground, such as the Supreme Court in Roe v Wade (1st trimester), while others lie at the opposite pole.

For centuries, governments have attempted to control the behavior of citizens through religion and the use of fear and guilt. Historically, in Europe, it was the duty of religious leaders was to indoctrinate parents in what the government considered proper behavior, and the duty of parents to indoctrinate their children with the church's beliefs. The church's morality was the morality of society. If one person went astray, and failed to follow the rules, they would be subject to social judgment, become outcasts. If being social outcasts did not work, governments had other methods of control.

Throughout history, governments have hung, imprisoned, tortured or otherwise punished any who violate the country's existing moral standard.

Think about it. We, in the United States, still live in the remnants of the past. Social judgment is everywhere, and traditional marriage was at its core, with women being its primary keepers, with their greatest judgments reserved for other women. If a woman had sexual relations with multiple partners, she was a (insert expletive here). If the woman had a child by a man not her husband, she was a (insert expletive here).

Things change, and in today's society, they change faster than ever. Fifty years ago, an eighteen-year-old could go to jail for having sex with his seventeen-year-old fiancée. Today, we would laugh at that definition of statutory rape. Most states have eliminated that law from their books along with all of the anti-sodomy and anti-contraception laws. Heck, in Nevada, even prostitution is legal, and, of course, gambling has made a comeback in Native American casinos, riverboats and Atlantic City. States now have sanctioned gambling in the form of the various lotteries, all in the name of contributing to some social good, such as education.

Fifty years ago in the United States, failure to pay child support was not all that important to states. If a person failed to pay child support from a court order, perhaps the local prosecutor to look at it, but prosecutors would rather spend their precious resources and time, and especially jail space, on "real" criminals-- the ones who robbed, raped and murdered. Fifty years later, the federal government pays states, and most particularly counties and parishes, to employ prosecuting attorneys to put these deadbeat parents in jail. Moreover, the federal government actually pays the states for the jail space, so each county or parish might even make a profit.

Of course, fifty years ago, many states were fighting a losing battle for states' rights and the Tenth Amendment. So, how did this happen? The federal government made the states an offer they could not refuse. Take the money or lose your federal funding for welfare. This worked of course.

Given that change is constant, the only real question is how long might this focus last. True, the past fifty years have borne stronger and stronger focus on failure to pay support, regardless of cause. But remember that non-support was created in fairly good economic times. Nowadays, it is lose your job and go to jail. With so many people unable to find sufficient employment, and so many people simply financially unable, this huge federally funded monstrosity might not have long to live. Moreover, as we will discuss later, the System has borne smarter and better violators, just like prohibition gave us smarter and smarter bootleggers.

In the end, you must ask yourself the all-important question. Where is my moral compass? What is really my duty to my children? How best can I achieve that duty? Am I a parent or just a giant wallet as the Child Support System dictates?

People often say, the tighter the grip, the more that slips through the fingers. With the child support system, it is much more complex. Never before in history has a person had to do so little to be declared a felon. There is no act, no intention, no will, not even the belief that one is committing a crime. Yet, it is the moral equivalent of a car thief or a drug dealer--

criminals who are gambling that they can earn a living without getting caught.

Will society realize the costs of the system are not worth the results? The future is clear as mud, and the present is overwhelming for those in the child support trap.

STEP FIVE:
Understand Where You Stand in Society

      History shows that any personal behavior can be justified, even murder. Thirty years ago, it was the Burning Bed Syndrome. A woman claimed she had to kill her husband because he was so abusive. A jury bought her story of abuse, and the case will live on forever, studied in classrooms and preserved in film. The question is not whether you agree with her defense, but whether you grasp its meaning and ramifications. Similarly, there was a recent story concerning a white security man who killed a person on the street he believed to be a criminal, who also happened to be a black person. At first, he was a hero, and would not be prosecuted; however, community pressure and talk of racism put him in jail and made him a criminal. . Funny, how things change so quickly.

Moral equivalence is the ability to be free from social punishment for an act that would ordinarily meet with prosecution. The best example is the dropping of the atomic bombs on Japan. During the sixty-seven years since the end of World War II, the common belief swung from absolute justification to those who claimed the then leaders of the United States were murderers of innocent civilians. Invasion of Japan would have resulted in American deaths of between 500,000 and one million--with at least as many dead Japanese. So, killing a couple of hundred thousand civilians was justifiable because it saved millions of others, especially since the U.S. was already fire-bombing Tokyo and murdering hundreds of thousands of civilians as an effort to end the war.

Another example of moral equivalence is how courts in the United States have applied the Bill of Rights. The Fourth and Fourteenth Amendments guarantee citizens unlawful searches and seizures absent probable cause. The Supreme Court created a rule that excluded evidence that government authorities gathered without a warrant signed by a judge unless there was probable cause that a crime had been committed. That same Supreme Court has interpreted the First Amendment to the Constitution to create a fundamental Right to Privacy. When 9/11 occurred, and Congress passed the Patriot Act, civil rights organizations went bonkers at the idea of special warrants. They also argued that foreigners, who were suspected of terrorism, were entitled to a jury trial, all of the due process of law the Constitution guarantees its citizens.

But where was the moral outrage when the federal government passed laws virtually eliminating the right to privacy and due process in the Child Support System? The silence is deafening. You see, terrorists and murderers are one thing, but failing to pay child support? That's bad behavior. Lock them up at Guantanamo and water-board them!

In the Child Support System, the government has achieved its own form of moral equivalence. Once there is an accusation regarding paternity and child support order, all of your civil liberties are subject to revision or elimination. If one volunteers, or is court ordered to produce a DNA sample because of an accusation of paternity, the sample and/or result are no longer private. In fact, if the match is negative, the government keeps the information in a database just in case there is a future match. Many a man has had a negative result on one test, only to find he has matched another case, and suddenly he is linked to another child. The moral equivalence: Establishing a child support order justifies this invasion of privacy.

Step back and think about this for a minute. The government spends billions of dollars a year on HIPPA, a privacy act geared to allegedly protecting your deepest secrets, but it is okay if they keep your DNA in a database. Are you starting to understand?

The Child Support System has one stated goal--collect child support, and collecting DNA is just the start of this process. Once a child support order is created, whether you are the person paying or receiving, the state agency managing the file has access to almost all of your private financial information. State workers have information about your bank accounts, your employment history, your personal employment records, and can use them to determine your liability or the liability of others.

Within the system, the federal government insisted that each state create an administrative agency geared for the sole purpose of creating, enforcing, modifying and punishing for noncompliance-- all without the right to a real trial, in front of a real judge, or even the right to actual judicial review. In the administrative child support system, the agency may hire one person who acts as case worker, and this person may have the power of judge, jury and executioner. The case worker has the discretion to determine whether proper notice was given, and whether any response was given or appropriate. Once an order is established, the same worker has the discretion to suspend driver's licenses, professional licenses, garnish wages, attach bank accounts, refer the case to the local prosecuting attorney for criminal or civil punishment, or do nothing at all.

In one of the most important cases in the history of the Child Support System, the Supreme Court of Missouri decided whether the state child support administrative agency could create a paternity and child support judgment without judicial review, and thus making the order binding on a judge and denying someone the right to challenge the issue of paternity. The Missouri Supreme Court decided that paying child support is the same as paying taxes. People just owe it. One would think that such a position would cause screams from civil libertarians everywhere, but silence ruled the day. After all, these weren't terrorists, or even Neo-Nazis who wanted to march on Skokie, Illinois, a place of large Jewish population. Those groups were entitled to due process.

But these are possible Deadbeats …

The Baby and the Bath Water

Back in the 1970s, social scientists determined that men who were ordered to pay child support were approximately 80 percent current on their financial obligations. Women who were required to pay child support were only about 50 percent current. Of the men who did not pay, the federal studies showed that about half were financially unable to pay, and about ten percent were intentionally not paying. About twenty-five years later, a new study elicited almost exactly the same results. The billions of government funding made no real change in behavior. It did not matter what new sanctions were introduced. The percentage was the same. By the way, the same studies found that women were only 50 percent current on their support obligations.

Politics won out again and the crusade against the evil deadbeats continued.

STEP SIX:
Understand That Girls Rule

One of the biggest lies is one that places women in the same category as blacks, Jews, or any other class that has suffered throughout history. For the most part, women have been the protected class, held on a pedestal. Early man revered and even worshipped women for their power to create life. Thousands of Greeks and Trojans died to protect the beautiful Helen. Men fought and died to protect women throughout history, or to bring back riches to feed, clothe and otherwise spoil their women. Let's face it, guys. They wanted to have sex, lots of sex, and let's face it-- no matter what the culture, the race or the place, men seek riches primarily to impress women.

For a more modern reference, how about the movie, "The Social Network." Sean explains, as a high school geek, how he founded Napster to impress and steal away the girlfriend of the lacrosse team's captain. The film ends with the main character fawning over the Facebook page of his former girlfriend whose wrath had inspired him to expand the Harvard Facebook first to her college, and then throughout the world.

But this is nothing new. In his book, "The Myth of Male Power," Dr. Wayne Ferrell goes to great lengths to document this female power over men. When Dr. Ferrell published this book back in the man-bashing years of the 1980s, it was a national bestseller, bursting the bubble of many powerful women's groups such as NOW. The book summarized and detailed how these groups had attempted to rewrite history to portray themselves as victims, when, for the most part, they were really in charge.

In reality, the theory was quite simple. Women were in charge of relationships with men because women were in charge of sex. They decided when, where and how. Men just wanted to have sex while women generally decide if they want to marry. Then they clearly decide when and if to have sex. If pregnancy occurs outside of marriage, women get to decide whether or not to have the child, or to give the child up for adoption, as well as whether or not to tell the father about the pregnancy. According to the studies of a female Ph.D. at Berkley, women make the decision to divorce 85 percent of the time, and contrary to the media, men having affairs represents a small fraction of that decision.

Margaret Mead, noted feminist and social scientist, said it best-- the woman's job in society is to train men. After all, women were the social creatures, and women decided what was socially appropriate and what was not. Just ask Carrie Nation, the sobriety queen of the 20th century who led the fight for Prohibition. That fight goes on today. Women could control men through manipulation. Men, on the other hand, could only control through violence. Again, this is an oversimplification. There were always exceptions, but without women, there would be no real definition of social mores, at least according to Mead. The word "civilized" has been thrown about throughout history as has the word "barbarism." In our culture, a civilized society protects women and children, and a barbaric or uncivilized society exploits them.

The root of civilized society is "traditional marriage." Marriage is a social convention of religious beliefs, but in practice, marriage exists to protect women. Divorce laws began hundreds of years ago in England as a means to prevent women from becoming public charges, meaning to require the husband to support his wife so the government would not have to. These ideas persist today.

Margaret Mead would be shocked if she were alive today. Without socialization, there would be no marriage. The uncivilized male was geared genetically to spread seed wherever and whenever possible. Women were genetically geared to nesting. Marriage, in theory, bound one woman to one man, and made the man financially responsible to support the woman and any children she bore during the marriage.

This was a delicate balance for society. Since 1500, the rule had been the same. It was believed that women, who were in control of sex, should marry first to make certain they did not have children out of wedlock. Once pregnant, they could only hope the father would propose marriage, or at least acknowledge the child. Without marriage they would give birth to a "bastard," a child with right to inheritance from the natural father. Pregnancy was not something they could hide, and being pregnant and not being married was shameful. Legally, a man had the primary duty to support a child born during a lawful marriage, while the woman had the primary duty to support her child born out of wedlock. These heavy financial and social sanctions, together with the reality that women controlled sex, kept marriage intact and men at a distance.

The first attack on this social arrangement came with the creation of contraceptives. Society's greatest fear was that contraceptives would eliminate the sanction against sex out of marriage. Early feminists, and free love advocates, such as Margaret Sanger in the late 19th century, were a thorn in society's side. Religion, especially in the Catholic Church, fought contraceptives as a violation of God's will, even supporting legislation to ban them for married couples.

As a direct consequence, the world of 1962, at the base of the child support system, was very simple and straight forward. Social roles were entrenched. Men worked and supported their wives and families. If there were a divorce, the woman got custody, and he man paid child support and maintenance or alimony to the wife. Of course, divorce was allegedly hard to get, unless there was actual fault. The law of each state was different, and the Mexican or Haitian "quickie" divorce became part of the social fabric.

Things change, however, and in the 1960s, things changed quickly. First, contraceptive laws were stricken as a violation of the Right to Privacy. Then, in 1968, society protected the sanctity of marriage, taking another hit when the Supreme Court all but threw out all child support and inheritance laws that discriminated against the group formerly called "bastards." Then the drug and free love cultures and free love followed.

In the 1960s, women successfully gained--through the courts--Equal Protection for gender discrimination, opening the door for women to assume roles society had held primarily for men. At the same time, barriers against divorce began falling, until there was no barrier at all.

But a funny thing happened along the way. As women took more and more male roles, men became more and more involved with their children. Soon, the "tender years" presumption was gone. In divorce, the every other weekend visitation for men became two days a week, three days a week, or fifty/fifty. More men were gaining custody of their children in divorce more often, than in almost one hundred years, when the children were considered their property. In divorce, and with children born out of wedlock, states began passing laws presuming joint custody.

Sometimes change happens too quickly. In 1962, the year of the unofficial creation of the child support system, it was the ideal of a great majority of young women to marry, to marry well, to have a home and children to raise, all while their husbands went off to work and supported them. Back in the 60s and 70s, many women went to college primarily to get their "Mrs." Degrees to find husbands. While some really sought careers to take advantage of Equal Protection, the old fashioned ideas that the man was primarily financially responsible, and the woman should be protected, still survives in our state courts and child support administrative agencies.

Fifty years of dramatic change did not alter the presumption in the minds of men, women and judge's alike. Equal Protection should have awarded men custody more often, as it did, but women pay child support or maintenance? If women got custody, of course, they should be awarded child support. While if men got custody, the presumption was--"I gave him my child, what else does he want?" Many judges still reflect these attitudes, bending over backwards for wives in an alimony or child support cases, or for mothers in an out-of-wedlock cases, and finding a way not to assess child support in father custody cases. As stated earlier, of those women who were required to pay child support, the nationwide payment average is only 50 percent, compared to 80 percent when men are required to pay.

After all, the Women's Movement was not about married women but about women who did not want to live in the "Leave It To Beaver" generation. Many women still believe they deserve it all, equal protection, to be put on a pedestal, and to be supported financially.

So, men who are in the Child Support System are up against formidable obstacles. They must face the financial prejudice of the past, judges who still hold these prejudices, and from women who want it all.

STEP SEVEN:

Understanding Rights and Responsibilities

Someone has to be financially responsible--this is the mantra of the Child Support System. To the federal government, everything else is irrelevant, and every change that has occurred in the System since its inception is geared to achieve that outcome. Due Process be damned; rights of the child be damned.

Think of a rhino, blindly charging forward, knocking down everything in its path, mindless of the unintended consequences of its actions.

The effect of this federal directive can be devastating for men and women, as well as the child involved. The stated purpose of the Federal Office of Child Support Enforcement is to establish support orders, and establish paternity for the benefit of the child, but actions speak louder than words. In reality, the System is all about politics, bureaucracy and good intentions.

In the Child Support System, the federal government has been making it easier and easier for state offices of child support enforcement, and state administrative agencies, to establish support orders. Traditionally, it was left up to the courts to establish paternity, as well as determine custody and support. Administrative agencies are not courts. They are created from the executive branch of government and their power is limited. Administrative agencies cannot establish paternity; they can only recognize paternity by statute.

Historically, it was well-recognized that a child born during a lawful marriage was presumed to be the husband's. The presumption was one of the strongest in the law.   If a child was born to an unmarried couple, the natural father's name could not be listed on the birth certificate--that is until the system altered this rule after the Supreme Court created equal protection for these children in 1968. How else could the feds establish reimbursement of their exploding welfare payments? So, a man who has acknowledged his paternity in a notarized affidavit could "enjoy" the presumption of paternity.

It is important to note here the effect of the presumption. In custody fights, especially dealing with the police and the criminal system, the husband enjoyed the same legal rights to a child as his wife. However, the father of a child born out of wedlock may have a different level of rights, or no rights at all, depending on the police and the prosecuting attorney. For example, if a child happened to be residing exclusively with the father, whose name was on the birth certificate, and the mother, after years of absence, suddenly demanded the child to be returned, it was not uncommon for the police to charge and even jail the father if he refused to do so. Prosecutors might also charge him with kidnapping his own child, even though no court order existed.

In the early 1980s, the child support system permitted administrative agencies to establish support orders against any man who was presumed to be the child's father. The statutes stated that the support order established paternity "for all legal purposes." Logically, this meant the effect of an administrative support order was to give the natural father the equivalent legal rights of the mother. And since an administrative support order did not award custody, no one had custody. This came as quite a shock to the parents who were receiving support, especially the mothers, who most likely believed they had custody of their children.

In addition to administrative orders, where there was presumption of paternity, it was the charge of each county/parish prosecuting attorney's office to create--with federal money of course--an office dedicated to establishing support orders. These prosecutors were, and are, prohibited from addressing custody issues. So, in addition to administrative support orders, there were, and still are, court orders establishing paternity and support, but not awarding custody.

Confused? That is understandable. Think about how things were in 1962, with the child usually living with the mother. The System is based on this presumption, and has not changed with the times. While the presumption of fact that the child resides with the mother might have made sense fifty years ago, it certainly does not make sense today, where fathers and mothers share parenting roles. Yet, administrative agencies and trial courts issue child support orders every day without a factual finding of the child's residence and without a custody order, simply assuming the child lives with the mother.

Confused? It is hard to understand, from today's perspective, how there can be a child support order without an order determining physical custody. After all, if a court declares a man the legal father of a child, the Equal Protection Clause infers he has equivalent rights to custody. In fact, the legal has stronger rights than the mother's husband who has presumed rights of parentage because the natural is now the legal father of the child.

Moreover, in order to make it even easier to establish support orders, the federal government passed a new mandate under the threat of termination of funding. Each state then obeyed. Under this new rule, each state was to change their laws to permit establishing paternity through an affidavit. Studies found that men (who believed they were the natural fathers) were very involved from with their children from birth until the age of one, where their involvement subsided, much like shopping for a new or used car.

Of course, the federal government insisted on safeguards. After all, if a person buys a used car, or borrows money, federal law protects him by requiring full disclosure of all information, and a full explanation of the exact consequences of signing the document. Under the 1997 mandate, the states were to pass laws that called for full disclosure of the rights and responsibilities of signing the paternity affidavit. Here's the rub-- the mandate didn't tell the states exactly what they should disclose, but left it up to the states, which had no incentive to protect the signers. The result was sheer anarchy. Most states left it up to their administrative offices of child support enforcement to create the information forms. This was sort of like putting the cat in charge of guarding the canary. The result was a laughable system of due process violations-- all in the name of protecting the government's bank accounts.

Some states adopted a method where nurses at hospitals were charged with the duty of presenting legal documents to exhausted couples to sign just after delivery. How, you might ask, could a nurse provide legal advice? For the most part, the only legal advice that prospective signers receive, if they ever receive any, came not from an attorney, but from the agency itself. And, of course, the agency wants people to sign to make its job easier. It's sort of like a police officer allowing one of his fellow officers to act as your counsel when being interrogated. As a result, many times the legal advice is simply wrong.

In addition, aren't affidavits supposed to be notarized? After all, if you buy or sell a house, you have to show identification. The new federal mandate required notarization, or the signature of two witnesses. You could write down any name. It is quite unfair to ask, or rely on hospital personnel, to prepare legal documents. In the System, it doesn't matter, as long as someone signed on the dotted line.

Of course, these safeguards do not protect the rights of the child, as would be required if the matter fell to the courts. How do we know the person signing is really the father? In fact, the new mandate required states to pass laws that would permit a married woman to have another man, not her husband, sign over the child's rights to another man with the husband's consent. In the court system, most states mandate that the court appoint an attorney to represent the child's best interest.

The legal effect of this new statute is unclear, and varies from state to state, from court to court and from judge to judge. Under the new mandate, a court declaration of paternity is neither required nor permitted. But how can an administrative agency step over the power of the courts? For decades, courts have allowed this process to occur, and have excused the violations in the name of haste and, perhaps, laziness. After all, if the agency does the court's job, it is less of a burden on the courts, but most of all, it is the threats of cuts in federal funding that are behind this conspiracy. This was an "offer" the states could not refuse.

There are also the local police-- the foot soldiers of the legal system. Can the police arrest a man for kidnapping his own child, whether or not he is on the birth certificate? Mothers think they have custody when they give birth. Only the courts can grant custody. The same equal protection clause that protects women from discrimination also protects fathers from discrimination. So, no law can automatically give custody to the mother, at least under the constitution, especially if the state declares the father "the legal father" for all legal purposes.

Genetic Testing

Some states have taken a more tactical approach to establishing support orders, using the results of genetic testing as a legal basis for an administrative agency to establish support orders. Toward the beginning of the child support system, child support enforcement agencies would send threatening letters to men accused of being the fathers of children, and strongly suggesting their cooperation in genetic testing. At this early stage, genetic testing was as advanced as a 10K computer, and had many flaws. In fact, many statutes contain procedures to attack the test results in a court proceeding involving establishing paternity, while no such attacks are permitted under the administrative system.

Under federal pressure, states adopted a 98 percent rule, meaning if a genetic testing company determined there was a 98 percent probability of paternity, there was a presumption of paternity. Nowadays, testing is so advanced, that any test result that is less than 99.999 percent result is usually a zero. Under the old tests, lawyers could argue that genetic testing was really a test of exclusion, and any percentage of inclusion was simply a fabrication. Nowadays, science has made these arguments disappear.

Regardless, the key here is that voluntarily participating in genetic testing might allow a child support enforcement agency to establish a support order. The completion of that order may result in establishing paternity "for all legal purposes." Again, it is a support order without a custody order, leaving custody battles to the police. As well, once one's DNA results are in the system, one might be a blind match to other prospective accusers. Again, that could result in a child support order. No one need accuse. No one even needs to know the name. For science fiction fans, it is one small step for man, one giant step toward Aldous Huxley's *Brave New World.*

STEP EIGHT:
Child Support Inconsistencies

Some fifty years ago, federal prosecutors, and others within the federal criminal system, complained about the inconsistencies in the sentencing of certain judges. One rapist would get life in prison while another would get probation. These complaints led to a Congressional select committee and "The Federal Sentencing Guidelines." The goal was to get rid of the wild inconsistencies. After all, crime and punishment was supposed to be about deterrence, and for deterrence to work in a society, there had to be some expectation of punishment. The result was a qualified success. The Courts of Appeal finally had the ability to give actual review of sentencing decisions, and to reign in trial court judges who did not comply.

Years later, Congress got the silly idea that they could apply the same theory to child support orders. This was problematic. Not only were incomes wildly inconsistent throughout the country, so were expenses. The cost of an apartment in Manhattan could buy a five-story mansion in Iowa. Food costs also varied wildly. So, the federal mandate was that each state would create a formula for determining child support. That way, the state agencies could simply plug its numbers into a formula and determine the appropriate amount of child support. Of course, states being what they are took this challenge in their own way. Some took a simple percentage of income of the paying person. Others sought more intricate formulas, attempting to determine the actual costs of an intact family unit to determine the level of support, spending millions of dollars to do so.

Each of these states missed the point of the exercise. No matter how exact their formula may be, it was just a formula, and it might to apply to an average person in that state, but that person did not exist. In reality, one had a better chance of playing a weird game of pin the tail on the donkey and hitting the correct amount of support among thousands of numbers written on a wall.

The entire idea of child support was based on the 1962 vision of society. Fathers worked. Mothers stayed home and raised their children. If divorce occurred, the wife was entitled to live the same lifestyle as if she were still married to the husband. Of course, the husband could live in a cardboard box because it was the children that mattered, and the mother was going to raise the children. Additionally, the husband was lucky if he got the children every other weekend.

Then there was the problem of what to put in the formulas. If a person worked a second job or voluntary overtime to pay his bills, should you include that in the formula? What about expenses? School tuition? Health insurance? Day care? What if the parties were not W2 employees? What if they owned their own businesses and they paid their own social security? What about passive income, such as interest? What if they were unemployed? Then there are problems with interstate proceedings, second families, and forcing insurance coverage when the recipient would rather use Medicaid.

In the court system, judges are well-educated and experienced attorneys who are either elected or selected to answer these complex questions. Not so in the administrative process. While some may have college educations, the pay scale for a case worker is lower, and the case load is much larger than the average social worker. In the federal government's belief system, everyone is a W2 employee, or should be. In this system, the federal government permits state agencies to peek into the employer's reporting program for federal taxes, showing each employee's income. In this world, application of a simple formula is as easy as filling out a 1040EZ. In reality, it is a 100-page 1040 with fifty attachments. These case workers are given a wide berth in their decisions. The result is sheer randomness.

There is one constant: an age-old prejudice still existing in the minds of the decision makers--the man pays and the woman doesn't. So, judges and administrative employees across the country will bend the rules, and more often than not, the bend goes in favor of the mother and against the father. If the mother is the one who is supposed to pay support, they will find a reason not to grant it. If the father is supposed to pay, the numbers will be skewed against him. The same goes for husbands and wives in alimony cases. While these prejudices are fading away slowly with time, like racism they will always be there, lurking under the surface.

Snapshots and Modifications

The grand assumption in the child support system is that it will start when the parents and the child are still young, and then income will increase gradually over time as the child gets older. This was how it was in 1962, but it hasn't been that way for decades, especially today. People are not getting married out of high school and reaching their peak of employment when their children are finishing high school. Couples are having children later in life with many variables--perhaps earning their peak income when their children are in their young teens, or losing their job anywhere along the line, or experiencing dramatic decreases in income in their fifties, or sometimes even earlier.

Therefore, the child support system is now about timing. At the moment the order is entered, how much are they earning? What are their relevant expenses? What if a person paying support is unemployed on the date of the order, and then gets a fantastic paying job sixty days later. The support number would be artificially low in the eyes of the person receiving the support. Of course, the opposite could be true. The same goes for Motions to Modify. If the person paying is lucky under the system, that person will have the income years prior to any modification, and have the worst years during the modification process.

Remember, the theory is all based on the artificial idea of the 1962 family unit. If the husband made more, the family did better, and the family is entitled to live that lifestyle. This is a complete fiction. Many families earning the big bucks lived like paupers because they believed in investing or saving for the future, while others who made a lot less were more interested in impressing their neighbors and friends or and lived beyond their means.

Yet, the child support system persists on this fiction that men will make more money over time. Remember 1962? There was the belief that men who did not work were just lazy. This prejudice persists in the modification process with the idea that men who do not have increases in income over the length of their lives are not industrious enough. Therefore if they did not follow this fictional path, they suffered the consequences.

STEP NINE:

Understand Changing Roles and Legal Consequences

Many men do what they think they are supposed to when it comes to their children. In 1962, those duties were clear. Nowadays, these responsibilities could not be more unclear. In 1962, if the girl you were dating happened to get pregnant, your duty was to marry her, and the two of you were supposed to do the best you could. Of course, in 1962, having a child out of wedlock was an embarrassment, especially for a young girl. Marrying her was chivalrous-- the rough equivalent of throwing your body, as opposed to your coat, over a puddle and allowing her to walk across.

For decades in this country, marriage has been dying as a social requirement to have a child. In fact, except for a small minority, it is an afterthought. The child support system has created mechanisms to establish parentage without understanding its effects on the street. Socially, and through decades of psychological studies, we have learned that a father's role is much more important to a child than was thought in 1962. And states, through their custody statutes, have moved with the times. Many states presume joint caretaking roles. Many men have embraced that role, sometimes being principal caretakers in the relationship.

Left alone, outside the System, young fathers and mothers of children, starting in the 1980s especially, would work out these issues, using the principles of "the Golden Rule" that had guided their respective youths. This became a simple system of give and take. If the couple were married and/or living together, they would share duties that would have solely been the mother's in the past. Even those unmarried couples not living together would do their best to work out arrangements.

At the beginning of this phenomenon, young fathers would show up with huge boxes of disposable diapers and formula, and work out parenting times to help the tired mother. Later, as society adopted alternate weekends as a norm, so did these young couples. These couples would adopt what amounted to a rental agreement. Mother would think, "It's my child, but you could see your child as long as you pay." And, for more than a decade, shared custody has been more the norm, and that has translated to the street, and to these young couples. Sharing expenses is less important than sharing caretaking duties. "It's your turn" is more the norm. Young mothers worry about their fleeting childhood and to escape the confinement of parenting their children 24 hours a day. Moreover, these young mothers tend to recognize the need for their children to have a father in their life, and want this male influence. In fact, sometimes it is the young father who matures quickly and assumes caring for the child while the young mother prefers to go on with life as if it were one endless party.

Conflicts and the Cops

A generation ago, young mothers would think nothing of denying access of a child born out of wedlock to the father who refused to marry her. Perhaps those mothers witnessed wives would take their children, empty the house and move on with their lives without a thought to the impact on their children. A generation ago, many fathers believed they had no rights to their children, especially if they were not married. When there was a conflict, the police would arrive and arrest the man, or allow the woman to take the child or children and leave peacefully. Police, especially without a court order, followed the common belief of 1962 that the child belonged with the mother.

Today, these decisions are much more complex. Local police are on the front line of custody battles, and most often they are clueless, or they have an agenda. Sometimes they enforce court orders. Other times safety issues might interfere, even though they know that child abuse claims in custody battles are most often false.

Then there are those situations when there is no court order, and the child is born out of wedlock. Just two decades ago, police would arrest and charge men with kidnapping their own children, even if they were living with them full-time, if the mother demanded them back, and the father refused. This would happen even if the father were listed on the birth certificated. Nowadays, Equal Protection is in vogue, as well the constant threat of litigation, and that same police officer might take it to the other extreme.

In one extreme example, a young woman gives birth, and is breast feeding her infant. The natural father, who did not sign off as the father at the hospital, calls and requests to take the child for a couple of hours. The exhausted mother agrees. After two hours, the man has not returned the child. She calls frantically until she finds out he has no intention of returning the child. She calls the police. The police ask her one question-- is he the father? When she answers in the affirmative, the police inform her there is nothing they can do because the father has the same rights to the child as her.

Into this world, there is the matter of the 1997 mandates. Completing the affidavit establishes paternity for all purposes. In essence, the man is the legal father even if he is not the biological father; he has the same rights as the mother. So, no wonder police are hesitant. Of course, this leaves many parents in complete chaos. Remember, under this scheme, if there is just a child support order, there is no custody order, and thus no one has custody.

Interstate Battles

The right to travel has been in conflict with the best interest of the child since custody battles began. The results of these battles vary from state to state and even judge to judge. The states have adopted similar versions of an interstate compact on how to determine the court of jurisdiction. The rule is too complex to discuss here.

Nevertheless, the one thing you need to know is that absent a court order for custody, nothing prevents a parent from removing a child and relocating to another state. Once the child has moved to another state, it is difficult, and sometimes impossible to force the parent to move back. And most important, remember a child support order is not a custody order. So a parent receiving support can move with the child, and can also establish, enforce or even modify the child support order from across state lines.

STEP TEN:
The System Punishes "Good Dogs"

Dr. Laura Schlesinger, noted radio psychologist, has a favorite saying: "No good deed goes unpunished." In reality, the saying should be: "No good deed goes unpunished but simply creates an expectation of more good deeds."

Ask any married man. It's an early Sunday morning... you wake up early with a lot of energy and decide to surprise your wife with a spectacular breakfast in bed. She is so excited she rewards you with a morning you will never forget. So, the next Sunday, you set your alarm. The result is similar, but not as great. The next Sunday, you are exhausted and sleep in. She wakes up and kicks you. "Where's my breakfast?"

I believe the best illustration of Margaret Mead's system of socializing men comes from the script of an old movie. In the story, a young bride asks her mother how to be a good wife. The answer was not to love, honor and obey. The answer was a book. The book was titled "How to Train Your Dog." The mother instructs her daughter: "Just substitute husband where it says 'dog.'" In the movie, the young bride rewards her husband with a reward, a kiss, for doing something for her, and punishing him, withholding affection, when he does something bad. The movie paints men as uncomplicated dupes, doing good deeds to please their precious females.

In the Child Support System, however, good deeds are expected, not rewarded. The child support system presumes bad behavior. All stick; no carrot.

But it is not just any good deed. The deeds must be done their way.

Whenever a custodial parent obtains any form of public assistance, or requests the state to establish a support order, or when a court enters an order and services are requested, the system is engaged. Any prior agreements between parents are now void and useless. Whenever a custodial parent accepts assistance, it assigns the right to collect support directly to the state. This means the parents of the child are no longer in charge of the financial support. The state is in charge. This is sort of like when the juvenile court takes jurisdiction over a child.

Of course, nothing prevents the custodial parent from accepting cash or other support for the child that may seem like fraud, and technically it is fraud, but the government doesn't really care. The system presumes it is a gift. It does not matter that the non-custodial parent was never even aware the state has been providing support. Nor does it matter if the mother is receiving public assistance for five children, and four of them are avoiding the system. The state presumes you are responsible for 100 percent of cash payment paid to the mother for all five children. All payments or other support that the non-custodial parent provides for the child is a gift, that is, in the eyes of the system. This is because the object of the system is to obtain reimbursement. The math does not matter, or the numbers that show the actual reimbursement does not even come close to covering the cost of the system.

So, if a non-custodial parent spends thousands of dollars in support, takes care of the children for half the time, buys the children anything they want, it does not matter to the state. That's all a gift. The non-custodial parent still owes the state every dime it pays out, or every dime the state determined is owed to the custodial parent.

As you learned in Step 3, your morality is irrelevant to the system, and past generations set high moral standards that the system legislates and demands. Perhaps, you have such a moral standard. You have goals, excel at school, graduate with honors, and get a good job at a decent company. You want to provide an appealing lifestyle for your child. All of that is wonderful.

Things change however. You end up in the System. Maybe you marry and get divorced. Perhaps, you are in the administrative system. It doesn't matter. An arbitrary number is set and the federal government requires your state set a number. Then, you continue to do well, receiving a promotion and a raise. The custodial parent requests or files that modification looking for an increase. You might even agree to one. After all, you have a good job and you can afford it. Your children are your number one priority. You are being a good dad in the eyes of the system. Custody doesn't matter. You could have the children half the time, or mother of your children could have run off with the children and is living across the country, or you may choose not to see your children. The system does not care. You pay what the system demands because you are a "good boy."

Suddenly, your company goes belly up. The market you have worked in no longer exists and you need to be retrained. Now you are unemployed. In the

"Leave to Beaver" world of 1962, you would suffer and your family as well, but the system presumes you are a lazy bum. You still owe that money even though it was not your fault you lost your job. Remember the system is based on a time when salaries went up over time, not down.

You have the right to file for a modification, but that costs money. You need to hire a lawyer, but what if you get a new job before the modification comes through? You roll the dice and pay a lawyer from your unemployment. Six months rolls by waiting for the court to hear your case. If you are in the administrative system, years could go by before getting your review. After a year, you get a new job. You are earning just enough that the modification is no longer available to you. Guess what? You still owe the same support for that year, even though you weren't earning anything.

Additionally, in that year, you could fall under the multiple other sanctions available to the state. The case worker could suspend your driver's license, your professional license if you have one, take your tax returns, take money from your bank accounts, or even refer the case to the local prosecuting attorney to ask a court to you put you in jail because you are behind on your support order.

Or, instead of a career, you are a hard worker. You want to the best for your family so you take on two jobs, and work lots of overtime to get ahead. Then suddenly, you get hurt or otherwise can't find a good job. Your family falls apart. You can't afford to support them so they leave you. A judge or administrative agency could assume you have the ability to earn more based on your employment history and "impute" income-- assigning that income to you even though you no longer earn that amount. You might owe thousands of dollars in support, until one day you might find similar employment, or not. Of course, if a background check on a prospective employee turns up information of a large child support arrearage, the employer might not want risk hiring that person.

The system doesn't care. The System assumes that all men required to pay support are bad people, who are just trying to avoid their legal obligations.

STEP ELEVEN:

The System Rewards "Bad Boys"

The child support system punishes good behavior and rewards bad behavior. In fact, it actually creates bad behavior. This is what is known in sociology as a self-fulfilling prophecy. If you assume a result in any prediction, you will get that result.

The child support system is a giant bureaucracy which employs thousands and thousands of prosecutors, case workers, and managers-- all trying to justify their existence, and sometimes their cushy government jobs and pensions. In order to keep their jobs, and more importantly to acquire funding from the endless government trough, they must justify their existence. They are all baby birds waiting to get fed. The one who looks the hungriest is the first to get fed.

The National Office of Child Support Enforcement has maintained it is essential, and has cited its collection statistics not only as a reason for its existence, but as reason for stronger and stronger enforcement measures. In essence, this office gives reason for more and more power, and more rationale to invade the privacy of individuals in the system.

Imagine the system as a giant tuna boat with workers using their resources to catch the most tuna with the smallest effort. When they throw their net into the water, all they catch are the uninformed, naïve tuna who don't know any better. But let's pretend there are really smart tuna, with the intellect of dolphins. Those tuna have witnessed others taken into the net never to be seen again. They realize the only way to survive would be to swim at the bottom, far away from the net. They watch as the boat's workers sweep up their compatriots and send them off to the cannery. Even if the boat's workers see them, they are not really worth the effort, and they move on.

Let's give this a little historical context. When the colonists protested the high taxes Great Britain had levied, Great Britain pushed the punishment button. There was no carrot. Sound familiar? The more Great Britain pushed this button, the more the protest escalated and so on. This circle of bad decisions eventually led to the American Revolution.

System after system of government proves this point, whether the criminal justice system, or the taxation system. In criminal law, the higher the punishment, the less likely it will be enforced. With taxation, the higher the taxes, the less likely people will pay them willingly, and, of course, higher taxes lead to more tax cheats. The more tax cheats, the more it costs in enforcement to collect taxes, and the harsher the penalties. Sooner or later, there is a public protest. Further, and most important, higher taxes lowers the incentive to earn more, at least above the table. After all, self-preservation is the highest motivation for behavior.

That is exactly what the child support system is, an out-of-control IRS, but unlike the IRS, it has no political base to protest. It is a bureaucracy that feeds on failure, and preys on the emotions of the public to "get" those deadbeats.

So, the increased punishment reduces the incentive to succeed, and creates criminals out of otherwise honest citizens who cannot afford to pay their support obligation. Recall the 1962 law that caused so many to go from honest citizens to welfare cheats-- all that law did was create an entire generation of welfare cheats. When the government did little or nothing to punish welfare fraud, welfare fraud became a way of life, sort of like the 55-mile speed limit created a generation of speeders.

In society, the street rules. With women, the street is like New York, with information moving at the speed of light. With men, it is like a small town in Kansas, moving at a snail's pace, but eventually reaching its destination. The word on the street is the only way to avoid of having your income imputed at a high rate is to never have that job. What's the point in trying to make more money and have a better job if the government is only going to increase your child support, and then put you in jail if you were to lose the job? Better to sell drugs and make some real money. Better yet, be a cocaine king and girls galore willing to have sex with you in exchange for a hit. You might end up with ten or more children, but you can afford it. Heck, in ancient times, sultans had that many wives and hundreds of children.

Or, perhaps you are the hustler type. You start your own business, but know if you report your income, not only will you have to pay taxes, but the government will have a number to use for your child support. Better to keep everything underground.

Or, perhaps you already fell into the child support trap, and owe thousands of dollars in back support for whatever reason. Why work above the table and pay taxes, and subject yourself to garnishment and the government taking your tax return?   In all these cases, the law of self-preservation wins out.

Or, maybe you are like the wind, the type the government can never find. You move from state to state, and they can't even find you to serve you. After a while, they just give up. There aren't enough resources or incentive to catch up to you. After all, you are dealing with bureaucrats and all they care about are numbers.

Or, perhaps, you are the really smart tuna, who hides in plain sight. Join the thousands who have committed social security disability fraud. Then, not only will you not have to pay the government, the government will pay you.

STEP TWELVE:

Understand "Street Law" is Not the Answer

The areas of child support and paternity law are extremely complex, and there are many misunderstood, and even unresolved, issues. Instead of seeking the advice of experienced counsel, many people turn to the street for answers. As a result, many of these people make serious errors in judgment, and get themselves into trouble. This so called "Street Law" is so powerful, that people sometimes seek legal advice, and then ignore it because they heard something else from their friends, relatives and neighbors, no matter how illogical or even off-the-wall. Here are just a few actual questions (complete with Street Law misunderstandings) and actual answers.

Q. I was told that the court cannot make me pay child support if I do not take a blood test (genetic test). Is that true?

A. No. The judicial system is adversarial-- meaning that a proper written response is required after service. Failure to file a response with the court might lead to a judicial admission of paternity, and therefore a genetic test is not required. Please note, however, that a state administrative agency might be a different question. Seek legal counsel in your jurisdiction.

Q. The father of my child is a bum and has never had a job. I heard from a friend that I could terminate his parental rights. Is that true?

A. No. The entire purpose of the child support system is to establish paternity as a means of establishing a duty of support, and to save the government its costs in public assistance. Thus, generally, the only way to terminate his parental rights is through a step-parent adoption, where your new husband would take financial responsibility for the child. Seek legal advice from an attorney in your jurisdiction.

Q. The mother of my child is committing welfare fraud. She has a lucrative business as a hair dresser, but is lying to the government. I heard that I can stop my child support. Is that true?

A. No. State child support agencies and their legal representatives are well aware of the problem of welfare fraud, but federal law prohibits them from stopping benefits, or even seeking reimbursement, no matter how flagrant the fraud. The only remedy for the state is criminal prosecution, something that is extremely rare. As frustrating as this might be, welfare fraud does not affect your legal obligation to pay child support.

Q. The mother won't let me see my child. I heard I don't have to pay child support unless she does. And, by the way, I haven't paid for almost a year, and I got this letter from the prosecuting attorney. Is that right?

A. No. This is not a rental agreement where you might have the ability to deny payment for noncompliance. While, if there is a custody order, your state might provide a legal remedy for an abatement of support for denial of custody, or visitation, this requires you to take affirmative judicial action. Seek legal advice from an attorney in your jurisdiction.

Q. The mother of my child left our child with her mother, and she is living a thousand miles away with some guy. My best friend told me that I don't have to pay child support anymore. Is that true?

A. Probably not. Generally, a custodial parent, even if there is a custody order, has the right to leave the child with whomever they please for as long as they please. Usually, the law assumes that a custodial parent is passing on the child support to the person actually caring for the child, like an extended babysitter. Of course, nothing prevents you from seeking custody of the child yourself. Get a good lawyer in your jurisdiction.

Q. During my separation from my husband, I had a child with another man. Now we are through and I want him to pay child support. He says that he doesn't have to pay me a dime. Is that true?

A. No. I assume from your question you did not take advantage of the affidavit procedure where the natural father and your husband acknowledged the paternity of the natural father. If that is so, the way to get there might be complicated and even expensive. Legally your husband is presumed to be the father of the child. The only way to make another person pay child support is to get a genetic test through a state child support agency or the court. The court system will probably appoint an attorney to represent the best interests of your child. Get a good divorce attorney. That way you can kill two birds with one stone.

Q. I had sexual intercourse with my boyfriend, but also had sex with his twin brother. I am not sure which one is the father. I heard I can choose which one to make the father. Is that true?

A. Maybe. From your question, I assume you understand that the genetic markers for identical twins are, well, identical. But, believe it or not, there was a case in Missouri with those exact facts. Since it is the purpose of the child support system to make someone responsible, the court has to find a way to choose. In that case, the mother testified that she recalled when she was ovulating, and which one she was having sex with at the probable period of conception. The trial court accepted her explanation, and the Court of Appeals did as well. Get a real good attorney in jurisdiction.

Q. From a man who lives in a state with a conditional termination of child support at age 18: I heard my child is not attending secondary school, so I can stop paying my child support, right? A guy at my work told me so, and he's real smart, so that must be true.

A. Probably not. Generally, it is up to the person seeking termination to prove the negative; it is not up the to the person receiving support to prove that the legal conditions for support are continuing Ironically, if a child's parent has died and the child is receiving Social Security benefits as a result, it is the child's burden to prove to the government that he or she is still eligible for benefits after the age of 18, as those benefits also continue to completion of secondary school. Seek legal counsel in your jurisdiction.

Q. I heard that if I get 50/50 custody, I won't have to pay child support. Is that true?

A. Possibly. Federal law requires that states have gender-neutral application of child support guidelines.

Nevertheless, the past dies hard, and the child support system is geared to life in 1962. Thus, even if you earn an equivalent income of the other parent, don't rule out the possibility of paying support. While most states have adopted a parenting-time credit to custody time, these same guidelines might also presume that one parent will pay for most of the expenses, and is still in need of support, even though incomes may be equivalent. If you are earning considerably more that the mother, you will almost certainly be paying child support. In any case, seek legal counsel in your jurisdiction.

Q. My boyfriend is listed as the father on the birth certificate of a child from a past girlfriend, but we did our own DNA testing, and he is not the father. So, I told him he didn't have to pay the child support. But he insisted I call you. I am right, right?

A. Probably not. If there is a judgment from a court that he is the father because he did not respond to a claim, you need to consult an attorney in your jurisdiction immediately to see whether there is still time to get relief. If a child support agency issued the order, then he might be able to bring an action in court to relieve him of the duty of support. This is an expensive and complicated process, and you should seek legal counsel in your jurisdiction.

Q. The father of my child is behind almost $5,000 in his child support obligation of $400 per month because I am only getting a little over $100 a month. Now I hear that he has three other child support orders from three other women. I hear I can put him in jail. Can you help me?

A. Unlikely. First, federal law dictates that any child support collected through the state is to be divided equally among the four children. That same law indicates that the government can only take 60 percent of his gross income (but not more than 150 percent of the net support obligation). It doesn't matter that you were first in line. As long as the state child support agency is collecting the support for all parties involved, the agency will seize his tax refunds every year if he were to get one, but is not likely to threaten him with jail for nonpayment. A judge in a civil contempt case might have a hard time putting him jail, because he is actually paying support and there are other children involved.

Q. I have three child-support orders and I pay them directly because I have my own business. But business has been bad and I have been struggling to pay my support. One of the mothers is married with a mansion in the suburbs and doesn't need my money. So I just thought: if I paid the other two who needed the money, it would be all right. But now I got this letter from the prosecuting attorney …

A. It's too bad you didn't ask me before you made this decision. You do not get to decide which of your children deserves your financial support. If you were a W-2 employee, the government would decide the percentage of your income paid. But since you are self-employed, the child support agency does not have access to your financial information, or necessarily believe it even if it did. If you failed to pay support for twelve consecutive months, the prosecutor could charge you with a felony. You should consult a criminal law attorney and a good child support lawyer in your jurisdiction.

Q. After seven years of trying, I finally got the state child support agency to issue a child support order against the father of my child. He has been getting her every other weekend for years and now he won't give her back. The police tell me they won't help me. They tell me he's the father and it is a civil matter. I don't understand. The child support order says the child is in my custody, but the police want a court order saying I have custody. They're wrong, right?

A. No. They are right. Without a court order granting custody, police have nothing to enforce. A child support order is not a custody order. Years ago, things might have been different. The police might arrest a father with whom the child had been living for years if he refused to return the child to the mother upon her request. But nowadays police realize you can't arrest a man for kidnapping his own child unless it is violating a court order for custody. If they did, he might be able to file suit in federal court for violation of his civil rights. The news gets worse. If the father of your child were to show the state agency he now had the child living with him full-time, he could ask them to enter a child support order against you.

Q. I have an administrative child support order. I was getting my child every other weekend by agreement with the mother. Now she met some guy online and she moved 3,000 miles away. I heard that I can stop my child support. Is that right?

A. No. Under the United States Constitution, the mother has the right to travel. Since there was no custody order, you have no right to stop support. But it might not be too late to start a custody case in court. Consult a lawyer in your jurisdiction.

Q. I met the father of my child when we were serving in the military overseas. He is very wealthy and I think he should financially support the child, but he left the military and is living abroad. Everyone is telling me I am out of luck. Is that true?

A. Not necessarily. The United States and other nations of the world have entered into an agreement to permit international litigation, including for paternity and child support. Consult an experienced attorney in your jurisdiction.

Q. My former wife has disappeared with our child. My income has decreased dramatically, and the state agency told me that they cannot modify my support obligation because they cannot find her. Is that true, and if so, what can I do about it?

A. It is true. The United States Constitution requires personal service for a court or administrative agency to enter or modify a paternity or child support order. So, if the agency cannot find her, the agency cannot modify the order. The only possible solution is to seek a change of custody of the child. Unlike support, custody is a legal status, and does not require personal service; therefore, you can serve her through a legal publication process. Seek an experienced family law attorney in your jurisdiction for more information.

Q. My husband is on a tour of duty in Afghanistan. He has been in the reserves my entire life. Just before my last deployment, he was working as a stockbroker earning three times triple figures, and he owed his ex-wife $10 grand a month in support and alimony. When he called into active service, I tightened my belt and we lived with less. He was in the reserves and called into active service during his first marriage, so I know his first ex did the same. He just got a letter from the state child support agency stating he owes more than 50 thousand dollars in back support. Can this be true?

A. Yes. Whether he is in the army or in prison, or takes time out from work to care for your dying parent, his support continues to accumulate even though he no longer earns the income at his employment. Thus, it is like a temporary layoff. While the nation applauds his service, the

Child Support System does not. It assumes that he
intentionally lowered your income to avoid paying support.

II. SURVIVING

THE TRAP

"Failing to prepare is preparing to fail."
John Wooden

Make no mistake. In life, there are winners and there are losers. Winners plan. Losers complain and moan. Winners understand it is war, and everything is fair in war, as in love. Losers look to their friends and cry "cheater" or "unfair."

The lessons of the twelve steps are simple and straightforward. Life is about a series of concentric circles, each circle being closer to a single person or close-knit family unit. The broader circles are friends, family and eventually our larger groups, such as our faith, our country and our world. In the child support system, the priority must be the very inner circle. No one else is going to help. You cannot trust the government. You cannot trust the courts (another part of government). You cannot trust reason. You cannot trust fairness. You can only trust yourself.

Before returning to the ten questions at the beginning of this book and in engaging the child support system, understand the basic facts of life. Relationships are perpetual, especially if you share a child, much less have ever been married. How two people in a relationship treat each other does not change, before or after litigation. Litigation is not the beginning nor is it the end. It is only a means to an end. Winners use litigation to get what they want, and get control in their lives. The level of that control depends on the individual. Sometimes, especially in divorce cases, the ultimate victory is to destroy your adversary.

Most divorce attorneys claim that there are no winners in divorce cases--there are only losers. Everything else is just a degree. Tell that to the father who will never see his children again because his former wife convinced their children to move a thousand miles away to live with her rich new boyfriend, all while he is stuck paying child support. She gets what she wanted, a man, younger and wealthier, while her ex-husband gets her wind.

So "winning" depends on your personal point of view, or perception. Many people judge their result based on the expected norms of society. For others, it is basic survival.

With these caveats and suggestions in mind, here are the answers to the ten basic questions at the beginning of Part I.

QUESTION 1. How can I plan out a successful strategy?

ANSWER: Be Proactive.

Plan, don't react, and do it at the earliest opportunity. If you have a child out of wedlock, start at the moment you find out about the pregnancy. Many people only seek legal assistance, and begin to plan when they are in crisis mode. Many people say things, or even worse, sign things without full knowledge of the consequences. Many bow to pressure, and make terrible mistakes, because they are walking in the dark, acting on raw emotion rather than considered information.

Even you have an arrangement with the mother, do no assume that this agreement is permanent. Things change, and sometimes things change quickly. She might get a new boyfriend. She might get a job opportunity out of town. Or, she might meet someone on the Internet and take your child and go. Remember, if there is no court order for custody of the child, she could take the child and leave at any point. The Child Support System will create and enforce a child support order from anywhere, but custody is subject to state jurisdictional laws.

Remember, it is much cheaper for you to act prophylactically, like wearing a legal condom to protect you from all the bad things that could happen. If being part of the child life is your priority, act quickly. She can get back support, but you can never get back the time with your child.

If saving money is your object, then follow the lessons of the twelve steps. Remember, there is no legal reward for doing the right thing. It simply creates an expectation. Sometimes, acting proactively can lead to saving money as well by forcing a favorable agreement. This approach, however, can be reckless unless you have quality legal counsel and advice.

QUESTION 2: What background information do I need to obtain to build a successful strategy?

ANSWER: Assess the situation

Pretend you are a general in the middle of a war. What would you do to prepare. The first thing you would do would be to assess. Where am I? How many men do I have? What are my resources? What equipment do I have? What about the enemy? Where is the enemy? What is the enemy's resources, manpower and equipment? Where does it stand?

In the System, it is never too late to act proactively, especially if your goal is simple survival. Any history buff will tell you story after story about an army that faced annihilation escaping in the darkness to fight another day.

Many take the easy road, even if it is foolish or even suicidal. It is far too easy to be a victim. Once you throw out those expectations of fairness and even rationality, you can plan a strategy to take care of yourself.

Last, determine, from an attorney, what you might gain in litigation, and what are the difficulties or possibilities.

QUESTION 3: What is the outcome that I want, and what is the outcome that will help me survive?

ANSWER: Assess your goals

What do you want? Do you want to be a part of your child's life? Do you want to evade the costs, or limit your damage? Do you want to advance your career? Do you want to just survive on the street? Do you just want to be left alone to raise your child without legal or emotional entanglements?

Engaging the child support system without a viable life-plan is like walking into the office of your financial planner without knowing what you want when you retire. At this stage, wash your mind of all the negative consequences and other negative thoughts.

Think about your life and what it will look like in a year, in five years, in ten years, in twenty years. Allow your attorney to help you plan to achieve these goals.

QUESTION FOUR: How can get my mind right to follow a successful strategy?

ANSWER: Eliminate the Emotions

This is certainly easier said than done since relationships, especially those involving children, are very emotional. There is heartbreak, deception, misunderstanding, bitterness, and even hatred, for starters. When assessing strategy, emotions cause mistakes. Everyone remembers the illustrious George S. Patton and his great victories, but very few know about his tragic, poorly planned attempt to rescue his son-in-law from a German prison camp. The king of planned assaults made an emotional decision, and hundreds of American soldiers died as a result. While no one is exempt, unless they are a robot or a Vulcan, you must make a clear-headed, cost-effective strategic decision, and you must learn to check your emotions at the door.

Relationships are emotional. When they end, someone feels a loss. Being pragmatic is difficult, not just because you have to deal with not only your emotions, but the emotions of others. Sometimes it is easier to hide than confront the other party. But mostly you must learn to look outside yourself, and see it as a game you must win.

QUESTION FIVE: What information about the other parties do I need to build a survival strategy?

ANSWER: Know your enemies

It is vital that you understand the goals of your adversaries. Just as nations build détente, you could do so as well. The United States and the Soviet Union found a way not to destroy each other during the adolescence of the Nuclear Age. Perhaps you and your adversary could do the same. Perhaps your adversary is dangerous, aggressive, unyielding, or mentally ill. You must know what they want to know how to proceed.

Getting the information correct is the key to successful planning. That is why the government has spies and the military has reconnaissance. The internet is full of resources. Use them to gather whatever you can to allow your attorney to guide you through to your goals.

Most important, however, is that you must know the persons and legal entities. You must know what they want and, as for the opposing parties, the emotions involved.

Ask yourself: What can I do to motivate or manipulate the situation to my advantage?

QUESTION SIX: What resources should I use to build and carry out a successful plan?

ANSWER: Obtain good and experienced legal advice.

Determine the "normal" outcome of your case in your jurisdiction under the facts of your case. Learn the best and worst case scenarios, the procedures, and the methodology. Find the best and the most experienced lawyer, and then get a second and third opinion. Just because that person is a lawyer, doesn't mean they know everything or are as competent as others. The key is to gather information to determine your course of action. Gather information about cost and see if there is a good "feel." Lawyers and clients are like couples. Sometimes they work; sometimes they don't.

The biggest mistake people is listening to Street Law and not getting the best advice possible. The next biggest mistake people make is assuming that, just because they watched television, they have the ability to represent themselves. Remember, this is a decision that could affect the rest of your life. If one doctor recommends that you need surgery, almost everyone would get a second or third opinion. Pretend that the decision on how to deal with the System is a life-threatening disease. Then you might do your due diligence in protecting yourself from infection.

QUESTION SEVEN: What information do I need to make a deal with the other parties that would be in my best interest?

ANSWER: Determine the Common Ground

Sometimes the best strategy is to enter a written agreement and make it an "uncontested case." Each party might get something from an agreement, and give up something. But equity, like beauty and fairness, is in the eyes of the beholder. Maybe you don't agree on fairness, but are more interested in saving the costs of litigation. Even after filing, a vast majority of contested domestic relations cases reach a settlement rather than going to trial. It is possible that a great majority of those cases started as contested matters because people did not investigate whether it was possible to reach an agreement with the other party prior to filing.

Nevertheless, in the mediation process, where parties attend a joint meeting in order to reach a resolution, this is not always true. A fair mediated agreement requires two or more parties that have an understanding of empathy for the other parties and/or is willing to give in to reach an amicable solution. For many men, the System interferes with this equitable process rather than promoting it by creating support orders without custody orders. For many women, the give and take that is human nature turns the child into a rental agreement, that is, no money, no visit. If the mother is already receiving money, either from the government or from child support, there might be a demand for additional compensation.

Sometimes, however, the mother needs help raising the child, whether it is what she deems babysitting, or just needs a break. While she might not value you as a father, she would be willing to give up time with the child for her own interests. After all, raising a child is a difficult job. Maybe she wants to share the load. In any case, this type of mother is ripe for making a bargain that could lead to a legally binding agreement.

QUESTION EIGHT: How will my financial status, and the financial status of the other party, affect my strategy?

ANSWER: Consider the Resources

In the 19th century wealthy people sometimes would be so bored, that they would make up facts to litigate just to see the outcome. Today, most people cannot afford the costs of litigation, but consider this. In the military, the winner of a battle or a war depends on the stockpile or production of resources. Money matters. Many a litigant has won a case by willing to outspend the other party. Do you or the enemy have family resources, and is the family willing to spend the resources necessary for victory? Other battles are won because one side is relentless in their pursuit. In war, and in litigation, relentlessness is an internal resource like no other-- just like the Vietnamese, who had fought for decades and were unwilling to accept anything short of total victory no matter the cost.

For women, the State cannot represent you, but represents its own interests. Of course the state's interests are not necessarily your interests. If the state initiates legal proceedings, then seek your own attorney, and attorneys cost.

QUESTION NINE: What formula should I use to formulate my strategy?
ANSWER: Weigh the Costs and Benefits

In relationships, the Golden Rule always rules. Mankind has achieved its greatness through cooperation, give and take. In the child support system, the government has disrupted this balance of nature. A man and woman who have a child together have two basic burdens, cost and caretaking. In the 1960s model, the man paid the cost, and the woman did the caretaking. When the government pays the costs, and goes after the man for reimbursement, the man has lost a pile of chips from which to bargain. The man then only has caretaking to offer. If a woman has that part covered, by staying at home or through family members or day care, there is only cost. Moreover, when the woman receives financial assistance from the government, the woman must sign an assignment of her rights to the government. Thus, the woman signs away her rights to make agreements with the man.

As a direct result of this assignment, the woman has "engaged the system," making it legally impossible for the two to reach a legal bargain. It is true that many couples raise their children without ever engaging the system, working out their financial and caretaking on their own. Sometimes the results, looking through the lens of the system, might appear unfair to one or the other, but these couples achieve their goals through their need to be cooperative.

The most cost-effective solution might be a bargain, like an "uncontested divorce" where a legal agreement is reached as to all terms, and then filed with a court making it a binding agreement. The solution might have problems if the parents live in different states, but that is for a lawyer to decide. In any case, you are buying the ability to enforce an agreement legally, and, once entered, it is up to you to do so. Most people respect the law, and will generally abide by a written agreement. Many will not. Many cannot, for financial, or other reasons. Some might enter into an agreement with no intention of abiding by the agreement, knowing the agreement limits their liability to the agreement, or believing the other person won't enforce it.

Then there is the third option, litigation. This is the all-out war discussed earlier. In family litigation, unlike all other forms of litigation, the two parties must live with each other in a sense before, during and after the war. You might choose this all-out war for several reasons, overwhelming resources, the impossibility of the other party, your needs and desire, no matter how rational, or perhaps, the choice was not your own in the first place. Regardless, remember as in war, peace can break out at any time, because, as in war, there is financial and emotional attrition.

All of these options depend on your ability to hire counsel, and to pay the costs. Sometimes, it requires family member to contribute or to lend money. Litigation is an investment in your future. The odds might be no better than the roll of the dice, but you cannot win if you do not play.

QUESTION TEN: Once I have formulated a survival strategy, how do I carry it out?

ANSWER: Make a Plan and Stick to It-- with Adjustments

Litigation is a game for the faint of heart. Litigation is not a game of chess or poker. Rather its best equivalent is the game of backgammon. The attorney is the player who continually rolls the dice. The odds of getting any roll are the same each time. Sometimes everything works out, and sometimes everything collapses. The key is to develop a strategy with your board, and stick with that strategy until something happens that might cause a flip or alteration of course. The examples are too vast to list, but let's say you are a father seeking some form of joint custody, and during the litigation, the mother is arrested for driving while intoxicated with your underage child unbuckled in the front seat. Your defensive strategy might reverse itself. Or, the opposite could occur, and so forth.

Another key is once you and your attorney develop a strategy, to keep on the same page, and act on that strategy, or worse quit the game. Many cases are lost because the client undermines the attorney through this failure. Of course, it is up to the attorney to explain and direct the strategy, with the client. Just as vital is for the client to shed his emotions, and act rationally. Clients need to know they are under the microscope at all times during the litigation process.

About the Author

Attorney Alan W. Cohen operates The Child Support Law Center in St. Louis, Missouri. He has been practicing law in the State of Missouri for more than 25 years. Mr. Cohen has authored multiple articles in the areas of child support and paternity. He is a graduate of Washington University School of Law and the University of Missouri-Columbia School of Journalism.

THE Child Support Law Center

For more information, please visit:

http://www.childsupportlawcenter.com

www.ingramcontent.com/pod-product-compliance
Lightning Source LLC
Chambersburg PA
CBHW051330170526
45166CB00002B/758